SINGLES, BEWARE
Before You
Say, I Do!

Keys to finding the Right person to Mary

By

VINCENT UZOMAH OBIBUAKU

Copyright 2022 Obibukau Vincent Uzomah

All rights reserved, No portion of this Publication may be reproduced, stored in a retrieval system or transmitted in any form, movies/drama or by any means: electronic, mechanical, photocopying, recording, or any other except for brief quotations in printed reviews, without the prior written permission of the publisher.

Dedication

This book is dedicated to God Almighty, without whom I would not have imagined that a book of this kind will be written by me; and also to my wife and Children. I own you a debt of love to be faithful as a husband and father.

To God be the glory.

Table of Contents

ACKNOWLEDGMENT

I sincerely thank all who stood solidly behind me to make this work a success, Rt. Rev'd Emmanuel Adekola now Bishop of Igbomina Diocese. Ven. B.O. Okafor, Ven. Rex Eze, Mrs. Joan Oji, Miss Roseline Ezediolu.

Your help and goodwill were invaluable. To you, I owe a debt of thanks for your cooperation. May the Almighty

God bless you abundantly in Jesus Name, Amen.

SHALOM.

Foreword

We live in a time when many families and marriages are facing the worst trying period. Much tensions, anxieties, quarrels, fighting, uneasiness and lack of peace are the order of the day. High blood pressure has become more rampant and people are dying young because of restless homes. More so, divorce and abandonment of matrimonial homes and children are on the increase. All these are happening before our eyes because of our failure to organize and manage our homes according to God's guiding principles and regulations.

Our youths are not properly guided hence they end up in faulty marriages.

It is a fact that the singlehood stage is very delicate and if misused or mismanaged could result to faulty and unpleasant future.

In this book the author has written some precious nuggets about 'getting into marriage' which if they are carefully considered will lead any bachelor/spinster into marriage blissfulness. It is written with utmost clarity and simplicity which makes it lucid, relevant original and authoritative.

I wholeheartedly recommend this powerful book to every family, bachelor, spinster as a road map to a happy home.

+Duke Kubwa

Preface

The Heavens and the Earth are held by the wisdom of God, so that both cannot collide. The world and the people in it are also a product of God's wisdom. So says the Holy Book. That sounds wise. "Wisdom is supreme; therefore, get wisdom. Though it cost all you have, get understanding. Esteem her and she will exalt you; embrace her, and she will honour you." Prov.4:7-8 *[NIV]*

A wise woman once said, "Being single is one of life's oft neglected joys." Which wise woman, you may ask? Me. And how did I come up with this invaluable golden nugget, you may further ask? Because I have been single a long time and am as happy as a woman can be. Don't get me wrong. I am not one of those who are allergic to romance or despise couples walking hand to hand with the one they love on the street, oblivious to the world. If anything, I find it endearing. I love the idea of love. But what I love far more is the idea of being single.[1]

---

[1] https://www.shethepeople.tv/home-top-video/8-reasons-you-should-embrace-your-singlehood-with-joy/

Singles, beware! Because the stage of singlehood is delicate, the misuse or mis-management of this youthful age could lead to sorrowing, regret and even death. Singlehood is a period when we look out for someone to fill our loneliness. A time of utmost freedom. Freedom to everything one wants in life. Choice of lifestyle to imitate, career to choose, spouse. This liberty makes single-hood the best, because it gives the opportunity to align to what matches one's behaviour or thoughts line.

Singlehood can be an assertion of your desire to remain a lone wolf for as long as you want. It gives out a subliminal message that you're willfully in-charge of your sexuality, body, emotions, and life decisions.[2] You have the chance to choose whether to make or mar your future. What we are today is a result of the decision we took yesterday. Nobody will choose for you. Gone are the days when parents chose careers or wife for their children. That is the reason we need God's kind of wisdom to guide us.

When I was young and tender, I lived with these choice: fear God and live, disobey Him and face the consequences. I didn't know what it means to submit to the Lordship of Jesus Christ. Until I was 22 (twenty-two) years, the year of my conversion. I must confess that life has not been the same since

---

[2] https://www.shethepeople.tv/home-top-video/8-reasons-you-should-embrace-your-singlehood-with-joy/

then for me because knowing God was the best thing that ever happened to me. God's wisdom enabled me to overcome the challenges of youthfulness and singleness. The experiences and the challenges I faced within my years of single-hood gave birth to this book, to guide and encourage singles and the married.

VINCENT OBIBUAKU

CHAPTER 1

Singles, Beware!

If you choose to be Godly, off course know that Satan will fight back. One of the areas he engages in battle with the singles is marriage, choosing a life partner. And those who enter into it without seeking God's guidance, often finds it difficult to find the right acquaintance.

This is the more reason this aspect of choice making should be properly considered before one enters into it.

Often I find that women, in this era of speed dating where journeying through life without a partner beside you at all times seems reckless almost, scramble to search for that 'special someone'. And sometimes, in their haste to secure that partnership, end up making the wrong choices that cause distress and end in heartbreak. The prospect of having someone - your someone - with whom you can vent, laugh, cry, speak, and enjoy is fairytale-like.[3]

Most single persons we find today have their agenda. Many are on a mission for God; many are

---

[3] https://www.shethepeople.tv/home-top-video/8-reasons-you-should-embrace-your-singlehood-with-joy/

also on mission for Satan. Some have entered into all kinds of secret associations. When in a relationship, it's common for women to lose track of their own ambitions in the sway of love.

There is increased pressure of taking the likes and dislikes of your partner into account before embarking upon things you wish to do - whether it's a quick trip someplace or a job change. Since you're sharing your life with a partner, you might feel obliged to take their advice on things that don't essentially need their advice.[4] This is the more reasons you must put into consideration who goes with you on this journey.

Others involved themselves in so many things as a result of their search for fame/ recognition and some others whose hearts has been broken due to disappointments has allowed such pains to open a doorway in their lives. Satan who is always looking for such opportunities capitalizes on these and ruins their lives.

"The Lord said to Satan, "Where have you come from?" Satan answered the Lord, "From roaming through the earth and going back and forth in it."

---

[4] https://www.shethepeople.tv/home-top-video/8-reasons-you-should-embrace-your-singlehood-with-joy/

Job 1:7
"The thief comes only to steal, kill and destroy."
John 10:10A [NKJV]

When Satan sees such people, a little advice or invitation will do it all, and they will be initiated into so many demonic activities, thereby oppressing their lives through demonic oppression. Secretly they will depart from their faith, giving heed to seducing spirit, and becoming wolves in the midst of sheep (Believers), the family of God.
"The spirit clearly says that in lattertimes some will
abandon the faith and follow deceiving spirits and
things taught by demons." I Tim.4:1 [NIV]

They will be good-looking, fervent in spirit, doing the work of God, yet except a person sees with an inner eye it becomes impossible for one to be able to notice or recognize them.

They become the target of all the singles in the Christian congregation; everybody wants to have them as husbands and wives because they possess that fascinating attraction. And because of their Christian endeavour and fervency, which every good Christian will always look out for, they soon win over the saints.
They are out to ruin your home, mission, vision, dream, purpose of living, joy of salvation. Can you

imagine the gift of God which is meant to make one rich, is instead adding sorrow to so many homes?

If it is truly the gift of God, why has it now turned to a battle ground, a pain-staking union? Instead of a happy home, why has the man/woman whom you know as a good sister/brother in the church turned suddenly to a lion and lioness at home? Why has he/she who did not miss church activities when you met each other changed to Sunday-Sunday church goer after marriage? Something must be wrong; and you must trace it from its origin.

Mission is the joy of every new convert, but for many it has changed to something else, most especially after marriage. Mission then becomes raising of children, and trying to restore marriage from crumbling. Satan has a way of keeping people away with strategies to make them busy. Someone will ask, "Will I leave my family uncared for in order to face church business? Won't the Bible say that I am worse than an infidel?"

Why won't you be? When you have taken the load, which was supposed to be God's own, on your head, why won't it be burdensome? You have refused to cast the burden upon the Lord, who cares for you. Have you forgotten so soon how you started? Was God given a priority in the time you choose your spouse? Did you seek his face; did you hearken to his voice?

***"For I know the plans I have for you, declares the
Lord, plans to prosper you and not to harm you,
plans to give you hope and a future" Jer. 29:11
[NIV]***

"The end justifies the means," they say. Did you think about the end which you are facing now, whether it justifies the means? Did you actually give it a thought, where you would be, where you were going, before you made up your mind to pick who to go with? It is only the person who knows where he/she is going, that can pick another to go with him. Anyone who submits himself/herself to a visionless and purposeless person does so at his/her own risk.

A missionary does not stop his mission until he/she has accomplished it, no matter the hurdles. Have you decided to stop or quit your mission or are you forced into a strange man/woman relationship because of disappointments? Life does not stop because one is disappointed; rather be challenged by it. What were the things that broke the relationship? Try and put them back together and you will see reasons to live and start again. Are you already in marriage and have discovered your mistakes? Then there is still hope. What are those things you see as your inabilities or disabilities? Turn around and see ability in those disabilities.

You can still make it, if you can do it again. Invite God in your life and marriage. Make Him the head, build an altar of prayer for Him, and then cast your burden upon Him for he cares for you.

> *"I can do all things through Christ which strengtheneth me." Phil. 4:13 [KJV]*

CHAPTER 2

God's purpose in marriage

"Judah has broken faith. A detestable thing has been committed in Israel and in Jerusalem: Judah has desecrated the sanctuary the lord loves, by marrying the
daughter of a foreign god." Malachi 2:11 [NIV]

"AND there went a man of the house of levi, and took to wife a daughter of Levi. And the woman conceived, and bare a son" Exodus 2:1-2a [NKJV]

You must have at the back of your mind the mandate to extend God's dominion and authority on earth. As God is in charge of heaven so has He set us to be in charge and in control on earth. The marriage relationship is the divine authority on earth. Whatever the man and woman agree to enforce on earth will stand. When a husband and wife are operating in unity, Satan in particular is helpless and then the authority of God is established. You must not take as spouse a "foreign" man/woman. You must marry a believer, one who believes what you believe, and who loves your brethren. He/she must be one who is ready to enforce the same authority with you here on earth to the glory of God. *Neh. 13:24-27, Ezra 9:1-3; 10:9-11, 44*

A man from the "house of Levi" must also go to the "house of Levi" to find a spouse. Darkness and light have nothing in common because there are so many things that will come up after marriage, which will not give a believer the time to pray for somebody to change and become what they want him/her to be. So do not imbibe the idea of *I will change him/her after marriage.*

In those days it was easy to locate a Levite and you would be sure he was one, but today many appear to be sheep but are wolves in sheep's clothing, so it calls for one to be very careful who you call a true believer. We have many Christians whose hearts have become like those of the Egyptians; who secretly live like the Egyptians but openly live like Levites Exodus 2:14. We also have the Egyptians who have come in, in the midst of Levites; they live like the Levites. Jesus said, *"I know my sheep and they know me."*

Be careful of whom you join your life with. As for Moses, the Bible says,

"when he grew up he loved his brethren."
"LOVED HIS BRETHREN"

"Now when Moses had become a man, one day he went out to his people and saw how hard their work was; and he saw an Egyptian giving blows to a Hebrew, one of his
people. And turning this way and that, and seeing no one, he put the Egyptian to death, covering his body with sand.
And he went out the day after and saw two of the Hebrews fighting: and he said to him who was in the wrong, why are you fighting your brother? Now the priest of Midian had seven daughters: and they came to get water for their father's flock. And the keepers of the sheep came up and were driving them away; but Moses got up and came to their help, watering their flock for them.
And when they came to Reuel their father, he said, how is it that you have come back so quickly today? And they said, An Egyptian came to our help against the keepers of sheep and got water for us and gave it to the flock. And he said to his daughters, Where is he? Why have you let the man go? Make him come in and give him a meal." Ex. 2:11-13, 16- 20 [BBE]

He went out unto his brethren in search of their welfare. He was committed to see to his brethren's welfare. He was committed to protect them and he never lost sight of them and so the Bible says, *"we must be our brother's keeper."*

Moses did not know those seven daughters of the priest of median because he had not seen them before but he knew in himself that they must be members of his tribe and so he went to fight for them. Exo.2:16-17 you may say, he knew them because of the flocks. Hebrew people are known to keep flocks, but Moses and Reuel's daughters never met one another before now; it was the love of the brotherhood that moved him to help them. Besides, Moses did not love injustice; he was a man who loved righteousness. Those ladies did not know him to be of their tribe because they told their father that an Egyptian delivered them. Moses was not an Egyptian, so it was obvious the girls never knew him.

They were not ashamed to tell their father about the man who helped them; they did not hide anything from their father. Again, Moses was willing to help unconditionally. *"He stood up and helped" Ex. 2: 17*

He did not help them because they were ladies, the weaker vessels. No, he helped them because there was a need to do so.

He fought for their protection. He did not stop there but also watered their flocks. I believe that Moses did all these good deeds without looking for a reward. The fact remains that the right man or woman made for you by God from the first day of your meeting will be a helper to you; he/she will fight to protect you. Hear this, no matter how a man pretends, the spirit of pride will not allow him to descend so low as to help unconditionally. ***"The blessings of God makes rich and adds no sorrow"***

The girls could not but tell their father (vs. 19). Any assistance given to you that you cannot disclose to your parents is not worth it. Any relationship hidden from the eye of parents, no matter who is involved, is not worthwhile, so must be examined.

They told their father and their father trusted them enough that he began to look for the man. Maybe their father knew that such a man must have come from among them, and not just among them, but must be a very good man who loved God. Such a man was to desire to have as an in-law. Hence, he looked for him. It must come to a time when those who will be your in-law will begin to look for you, your mother in-law will love you even before you are mentioned to her; so also your father in law.

Jethro had never seen Moses even before he demanded that he should be brought. Remember when they met, Jethro did not look at or consider Moses' educational background, wealth or worth but I believe he thought in his heart, such a man must be good and God fearing and he asked them,

"where is he, why did you leave such man to go?"
Ex. 2:20

Everyone looks for a good man/woman, the man/woman they will be happy with; the rich cry in marriage as much as the poor. The reason is that they did not seek for the good man from the midst of brethren. *Neh. 13:23-26; Mal. 2:11.* Even if it were from the midst of brethren they weren't careful and purposeful in prayer as concerning marriage. Maybe they were motivated by matchmaking, beauty or even wealth?

Moses did not know Zipporah until she was given to him by his father in-law. Many who are married today cannot go to their father in-law because of the shame that they took the man/woman away, even when the parents were not in support of the marriage. If I may ask, is it not right for you to pray and ask God to convince your prospective in-laws even when they stand as an obstacle? **2 Sam. 13:12-13.**

"Do not be anxious about anything, but in
everything
by prayer and supplication, with thanksgiving, let
your
requests be made known to God." Phil. 4:6
[MKJV]

Anything prayer cannot do for you, you cannot do it for yourself. Prayer positions you to prefer the will of God to your own will. There are many ways which seem good to a man but their end is dangerous. Prayer makes you to be contented, makes you to get the best, as long as it is God you are praying to. The earth is His, His plans toward you are for good not evil, and He gave Israel the best part of the land which flowed with milk and honey. He will give you that man/woman that will make your home sweet.

LOVE UNDIVIDED
"And Moses was happy to go on living with the man; and he gave his daughter Zipporah to Moses."
Ex. 2:21. 1 John 4:18, Rom. 13:10

Moses was contented to dwell with Jethro's family. Do you love the family, even before their son/daughter is given to you? When it comes to marriage LOVE-LEVEL must be from both parents, anything less demands that you stop and seek the face of God. You deserve a glorious home. "So He gave" Love is the only thing that motivates one to give. **John 3:16.**

Remember Jethro invited Moses to eat with him. You cannot eat with someone whom you do not love. Because of good foundation which was laid in this relationship, it was not long Zipporah bore Moses a son. Hallelujah! You will know a man/woman who loves God even after his marriage. After marriage God still spotted Moses, as he went to feed the flock of his father in-law. What a love! And God saw him at the mountain, because he went to the mountain to meet with Him.

He did not stop praying and waiting upon God after his marriage. Instead he was committed to do the will of God and God was determined to search for him, though circumstances drove him away from his brethren. Anyone who is committed to destiny does not lose focus even when situations around do not look pleasant. "Condition made him to be feeding flocks," **Prov. 16:8; 15:16-17** you may think but nevertheless, he was focused and determined to have a successful end. You must have a successful marriage, in Jesus' Name.

A minister who is careless concerning marriage will be careless concerning destiny and failure in marriage is almost automatic failure in ministry.

CHAPTER 3

The process of finding A life partner

God must be allowed to choose for you. Marriage is God's initiative because He knows our destiny; He knows who can tolerate our weaknesses, character and future. He knows who can stand or endure our presence. A lot of people allow others to choose for them, and end up in regret.

[1] SUPPLY THE MATERIAL

Be consistent in worship, prayer, and positive confession for your marriage. If you love your life and destiny you will consistently release words and prayers that will make your marriage glorious. Women do not go for a man in marriage; it is the duty of the man to ask for a woman's hand in marriage.

"For this cause will a man go away from his father
and his mother and be joined to his wife;
and they will be one flesh."
Gen. 2:24 [BBE]

Even in the animal kingdom, it is the male that goes for the female; though the female could entice the male, there is nothing wrong with that. It is indignity and a disgrace for a woman to ask for a man's hand in marriage; the man is the raw material while the woman is the refined product.

[2] ONE UNIT OF IDENTITY

If you are not ready to become one with your spouse then you are not ready to become married. If you cannot identify with someone it is not safe to unite with such a person for the sake of marriage. Look at the person very well and be
ready to identify with him/her.

[3] BE SET FOR MUTUAL IDENTITY

If you have a divergent life or vision, then there must be a converging of purpose for life; otherwise there is no future. A woman must always line up her vision with that of her man. All the senses of the body are located in the head. *Eph. 5:22-23*

[4] LEAVING BEFORE CLEAVING

"Therefore shall a man leave his father and his mother, and shall cleave to his wife and they shall be one flesh." Gen. 2:24 [KJV]

A man must be ready to leave every attachment, emotional, physical or material, before he can cleave. A man must not depend on any other person to feed or clothe his wife. A man that allows his father or any other person to feed his wife is irresponsible. A woman should not marry and be emotionally attached to her people. Every form of dependence must be discontinued before there will be cleaving. Nothing disturbs cleaving like the third party interference.

[5] SINCERITY, OPENNESS AND HONESTY IN A SUCCESSFUL MARRIAGE

When you build marital union on a foundation of deception the result in the future is disaster. Don't deceive the one you love. Sincerity is a major key to longevity in marriage. There are truths that are hard but must be declared whether or not your suitor asks. Most especially when you are undergoing marriage counseling, make sure you tell the whole truth, because it will help save your marriage. Nothing should take the place of integrity, sincerity, honesty, and purity as long as destiny is concerned.

"For he that will love life and see good days let him
refrain his tongue from evil and his lips that they speak
no guile. 1 Peter 3:10

"The lip of truth shall be established for

*Ever but a lying tongue is
but for a moment." Prov. 12:19*

Shame is the outcome when insincerity is the game. Lies do not become truths no matter how long they have lasted. Lies and truth could run a race but truth will always overtake.

[6] DIRECTION

If you are a son you will lead in every area of life, and proof of son-ship is by the leading of the Holy Ghost. If the Holy Ghost is not leading you, you have disconnected yourself from the family of God. You are to blame yourself; if you enter into any marital relationship which God's hand is not in. *Rom. 8:14.*

[7] LEADING

To be led, you must be willing to follow. To follow implies keeping your heart in a clear state of mind, having no choice in the matter but trusting God in his wisdom to give the best. If there is a place in your life which you cannot trust God for distinction then something is wrong.

To enjoy distinction in life the parthway is instruction. If you hear and obey what God says, the world will hear what you have to say. **Prov. 11:14; 16:22-23.**

WAYS OF LEADING

1. *VISION:* It can come in different ways; dream, trance.

2. *INWARD VOICE:* Inward voice is a voice that is not audible but yet it speaks.

3. *INWARD WITNESS:* Inward witness is a witness within your spirit.

4. *AUDIBLE VOICE*

5. *TONGUES AND INTERPRETATION OF TONGUES*

6. *LOVE AND AFFECTION.* 1Corinthians 13:8, 12. This is likely the most correct means.

[8] SET A STANDARD

"And Abraham was old, going on in age. And Jehovah had blessed Abraham in all things. And Abraham said to the oldest servant of his house, who ruled over all that he had, I pray you, put your hand under my thigh. And I will make you swear by Jehovah, the God of Heaven and the God of the earth, that you shall not take a wife to my son of the daughters of the Canaanites, among whom I dwell.

But you shall go to my country and to my kindred, and take a wife to my son Isaac. And the servant said to him, Perhaps the woman will not be willing to follow me to this land. Must I necessarily bring your son again to the land from which you came?

And Abraham said to him, Take care that you do not bring my son there again. Jehovah, the God of Heaven, who took me from my father's house and from the land of my kindred, and who spoke to me, and who swore to me, saying, To your seed I will give this land: He shall send His Angel before you. And you shall take a wife to my son from there. And if the woman will not be willing to follow you, then you shall be clear from this oath of mine. Only do not bring my son there again." Genesis 24:1-8 [MKJV]

Abraham was very strict on the issue of marriage for his son even at old age. He told his eldest servant to swear an oath that he would not give to his son a woman from a foreign land. When you are ready to get married seek the face of God by prayer and ask Him to give you a man/woman who knows Him.

"The servant said "Perhaps the woman will not be
willing to follow me to this land. Must I necessarily
bring your son again to the land from which you came?" Gen.24:5

This is where many men have gotten it wrong. Many have stopped seeking. Some have given in to fate; others left the family of God and have gone to take unbelievers as wives, just because nobody agreed to marry them. You must not for any reason force yourself to a man/woman. If not, you will end up being a beggar all the days of your union, or use material things to lure someone to marry you. Some go even to the extent of inviting the assistance of native doctors, while others compromise their faith. The servant said, "Should I take your son back to the land where you come from, the land which he was asked to leave in order to meet the woman?" The statement does not look offensive but Abraham saw offence in it.

"For if after they have escaped the pollutions of
the world
through the knowledge of the Lord and Saviour
Jesus
Christ, they are again entangled therein, and
overcome,
the latter end is worse with them than the
beginning. For
it had been better for them not to have known the
way of
righteousness, than, after they have known it, to
turn
from the holy commandment delivered unto
them. But it
is happened unto them according to the true
proverb, The
dog is turned to his own vomit again; and the sow
that
was washed to her wallowing in the mire." 2
Peter 2:20-

22. [KJV]

He left the land by God's instruction so he had no need to disobey God even for his children; rather he said, "If it is God who brought him to this land who spoke to him, that unto his seed shall he give this land, he shall send his Angel before him." Gen.24:7 Abraham believed God and trusted Him that He was able to give him all that He promised, so he was determined to hope on God that the son's wife must come from there.

As long as your desire is according to the will of God, pray hope and be determined to get it and it will be yours. Do not take because of challenges in finding a life partner, compromise your faith.

POINTS TO NOTE

1. Do not marry a person out of sympathy. (Let me help him/her
2. Do not be manipulated by match-makers (Oh, we match each other).
3. Do not be prophesied into marriage; all prophesy is for confirmation.
4. Do not be pressurized to choose, whether by age, parents, etc. (It is a personal issue)

FOLLOW THE FOUR -WAY TEST

A. *Love Test:* No matter any other indication given you go ahead, and if there is no flow of love then, do not proceed. **1 Cor. 13:8-13. S of S 2:3-4**

B. *Peace Test:* Let peace serve as an umpire or referee to you. The very time you lose your peace, stop. If you are at peace, continue. Check your 'peace of mind level' to know whether to proceed or not.
"Be careful for nothing; but in every thing by prayer
and supplication with thanksgiving let your requests be made known unto God." Phil. 4:6 [KJV] S of S 6:9

C. *Conviction Test: "For if our heart condemn us, God is greater than our heart, and knoweth all things." 1 John 3:20; [KJV]*
Conviction is persuasion beyond confusion. You come to a point where you know whom you should marry, like you know your NAME.

D. *Time Test:* Every conviction takes time to be proved. Consider Peter's confession and denial of Jesus.

CHAPTER 4

Spiritual networking Of human life

"I say, then, Walk in the Spirit and you shall not fulfill the lusts of the flesh. For the flesh lusts against the Spirit and the Spirit against the flesh, and these are contrary to one another; lest whatever you may will, these things you do." (Gal.5:16-17)

Diagram 1: These fellows are carnal minded.

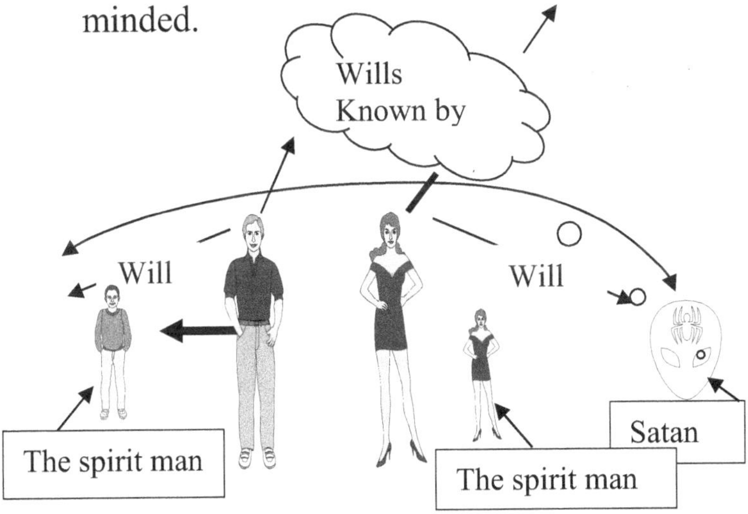

It is very easy for them to be man and wife

Diagram 2: One of these fellows is spiritual while the other is carnal minded.

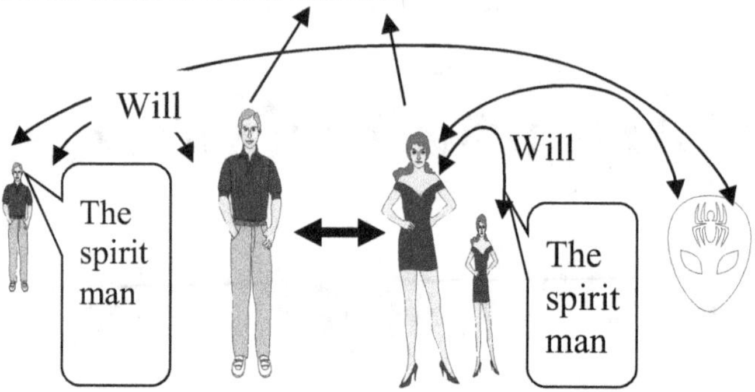

Satan manipulate the spiritual minded because his wills is known through his relationship with the carnal minded person, he oppresses him through masturbation and sex in dream. These forms a sign of agreement; and, if the spiritual minded person do not deal with the spirit behind these acts in his life, he may end up marrying a carnal minded person whose life is controlled by lust of the flesh

Diagram 3

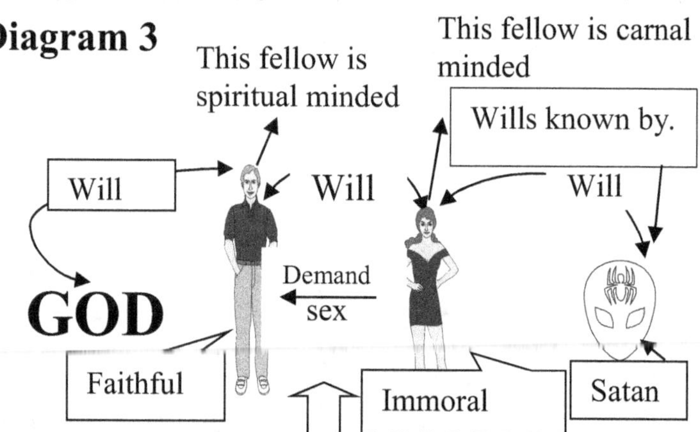

The spiritually minded person resisted both physical and spiritual forms of engagement / agreement by refusing to engage in all forms of immoral acts with the carnally minded fellow. The spiritually minded fellow's will is known as a result of their relationship, but there was no agreement to seal it due to the fact that he remained faithful.

Diagram 4: *One of these fellows is spiritual minded while the other is carnal minded.*

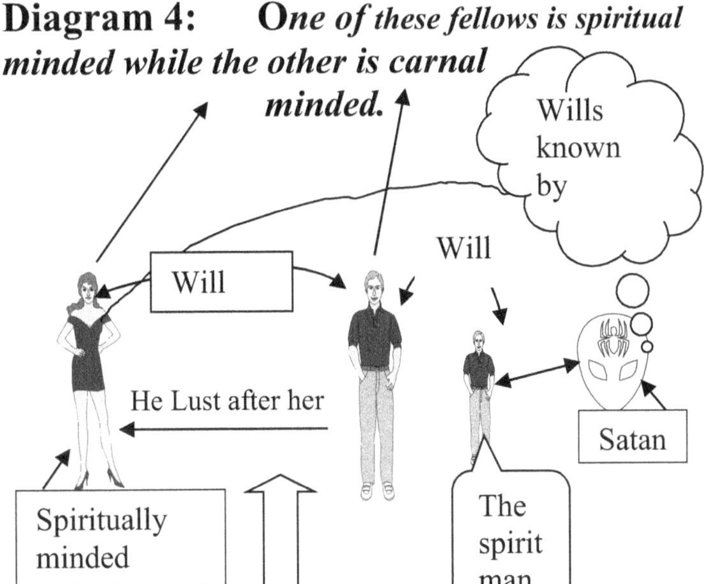

The spiritually minded person is manipulated through accepting engagement ring from the carnally minded fellow. This fellow also in his dreams saw himself marring her, and physically also had sex with her. In the realms of the spirit these acts forms agreement.

Diagram 5: *These fellows are spiritual minded.*

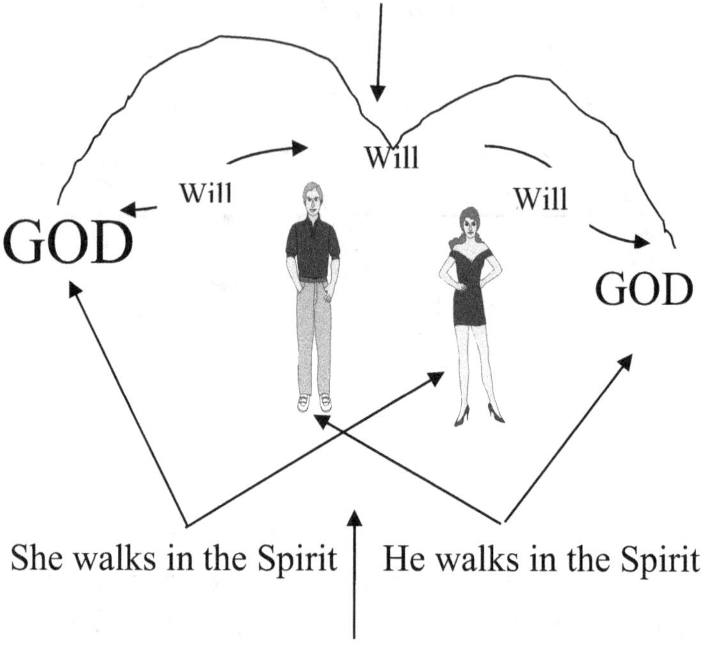

These two fellows are two Christians who 'walks' in the Spirit, as a result are not contrary against one another. And because they are spiritually minded, will enjoy life and peace, if they become husband and wife.

The diagrams explained Below:

DIAGRAM 1:
A canal mind has a spirit which controls his will and that spirit is not of God but is of the world (Gal. 5: 16), and when such a person comes in contact with a woman whose mind is Controlled by the same spirit, they both will flow well in a relationship because both of them are in agreement and are controlled by same spirit. Sex is inevitable in such relationship, because that is what binds them together in agreement. And such people can easily get married.

DIAGRAM 2:
A spiritually minded person comes in contact with a carnally minded woman whose will is controlled by Satan. The spiritual minded sees premarital sex as sin and refuses it, but the other fellow whose desire is to manipulate him through immoral acts goes beyond the physical to spiritual manipulations hence, she seduces him to have sex in dream /masturbations and through it forms an agreement with him spiritually. If the man doesn't resist her by praying when he is lured to do so, she will manipulate him into marring her whose mind is not

of God and there will be struggle in their marriage (Rom. 8:6).

DIAGRAM 3:

A spiritual minded fellow with a carnal minded Christian. The spiritually minded person's mind is known by the lady and she in turn reveals the man's will to her oppressor. But because the spiritually minded fellow is in intimate relationship with God, he refuses to have both physical and spiritual form of sex and overcomes any kind of engagement/agreement by prayer. Disengagement in their courtship is inevitable. Because two cannot walk together when there is no agreement. (Amos 3:3)

DIAGRAM 4:

A spiritual minded lady, who comes in contact with a man whose life, is possessed by Satan. Her mind is known by the man because she told him everything about herself. Though she resisted physical form of sex with him yet she gets engaged, weds and had sex with him in her dreams. These acts forms agreement and as a result she will be manipulated into marriage with him. (2 Cor. 6: 17)

DIAGRAM 5:

When a spiritually minded person comes into a relationship with another spiritually minded fellow, their wills are known by God. They both go to God in prayer asking God for His confirmation; if it will please Him to make them, husband and wife. God is the one who is to do the bringing together. Man's own part is to do the searching, being sensitive to His leading through the Spirit. (Proverb 18:22)

True loves can wait, in spite of orgies, lust, emotion or delay as long as it is to the Almighty God to whom it retires; I mean an account of whatever we do is given. So avoid any kind of pre-marital sex in whatever form. Be careful, for the power that influences what you do is what matters, so I encourage us to live in the Spirit so that we will not fulfill the desires of our flesh. (Romans 13: 10)

CHAPTER 5

Finding the Mr. Right

He, who finds means by which he is able to meet and marry a wife with God's help has found a good thing. This is not saying that you should go and begin to look for a wife. No, it says God will give you at His due time and when He does it must be when you are fully matured for marriage. He brings both of you dramatically close; it may be in church, office, market, anywhere. Something dramatic must occur to show God's mystery and His act, after which meeting it becomes a good thing. A man to whom a good thing is given becomes one who finds it.

**'Whoso' hath found a wife hath found good,
and
bringeth out good-will from Jehovah. Lord.
Prov. 18:22 [YLT]**

Marriage is a mystery because it is said that man's rib was taken to mold his wife, who was somewhere, where the man does not know. It takes the same God to do His mysterious act in bringing couples together notwithstanding the location where the persons are found. A wife is that good thing the Bible talks about. Many in search of this good thing have made mistakes; some married another man's wife while others married another woman's husband. This is because man has always wanted to go faster than God in everything he does.

There are so many men and women. If it has to do with you going up and down to look for a wife before the sun goes down, you will find out that you will meet a thousand and
one women who look good and attractive, but are all of them suitable as a wife to a man? No! If no, then it becomes imperative that God must be allowed to do the bringing together when He knows that you are fully ready and prepared both physically and spiritually. A wife is part of the things that make a man complete.

The Bible says, ***"He who finds a wife, finds a good thing"*** because it makes the soul joyful, it is part of what a man should have, as to make him complete because it is part of him. Do you know that a man/woman may desire to marry someone who to him/her is the best human being on earth? When there is a little misunderstanding you could see the ugly side of the person whom you thought to be the best human being on earth.

BIBLICAL EXAMPLES

The devil does not attack men without mission or destiny; he goes for the man that has a mission and a mandate to do something for God. He makes life miserable for men and makes the journey to their destiny look very far.

You can be taken down to Egypt because of what you carry but there in Egypt you are expected to make an impact, create a scene, and bring back glory to God Almighty. You are not to eat the king's meat in Egypt, because all their meats are not meant to favour but rather to devour. Joseph refused to eat Potiphar's wife "meat," (i.e. her offer of herself.) He rejected all that she promised if only he would sleep with her.

Daniel refused to eat the king's meat which was to make him grow fat, but rather consented to eat just vegetable and water. The king's meat will make you forget who you are, where you come from, your mission and where you are going. *Daniel 1:11-17, Judges 14:1-4; 16:1-2, 18-19.*

The devil is after your qualities; knowledge, skill, wisdom, vision, dreams. The Lord was with Joseph and he prospered; his master was blessed because of him, he also had success in everything he did. God made him to find favour in the sight of his master Potiphar, which made Potiphar to appoint Joseph as his attendant.

He also put him in charge of all that he owned; he entrusted them to Joseph's care to the extent that he did not mind any other thing except his food. What a favour! ***"The blessing of God makes rich and adds no sorrow."*** Joseph was well built and handsome and this made his master's wife take notice of him and said to him "come to bed with me." What a challenge to a young man of such character and fixture! Remember that the Lord your God made you the way you are, so you should show forth His praise and glory in the land where He has taken you. So glorify God with your life.

The enemy does not go to men who are worn out, but to those who have something to do for God. He wants to stop them, but I know that we are unstoppable. Joseph revolted,

"I cannot do these things! You are the only thing my
master kept away from me; everything he has is been
entrusted to me except you, why must I do such a wicked
act against God?" (Gen.39:9)

I encourage you young man, woman to revolt whenever the Devil or evil knocks on your door or you are enticed to eat the King's meat and sin against God. Any un-confessed sin multiplies itself to more sins; don't cover any act of sin so it will not lead you to commit it, *"Abstain from all appearance of evil."* **1Thes 5:22 [KJV]**

She kept on coming after Joseph and Joseph kept on resisting her. Do not keep any relationship that is not to the glory of God. Women will run after you and strange men will pursue you when you have vision or dream. Vision is a revelation of what will be. People will seek after you when they discover you have something upstairs.

When your vision begins to unfold, do not sell it or your dream for a momentary pleasure. Sin is a vision and dream killer and so must be resisted. If you love your mission on earth you must then keep away from those things which are there to kill your purpose of living.

PURPOSE
Discover your purpose in life and then look for who will help you achieve such purpose. Many people today have been hindered and cannot get to the goal because of wrong
association. When you associate with wrong people they will divert your vision in life.

"Be not deceived: evil communications
corrupt good manners.
Awake to righteousness, and sin not; for some
Have not the knowledge of God: I speak this
to your shame." (I Cor. 15:33-34)
"And Samson went down to Timnath
and saw a woman in
Timnath, of the daughter of the Philistines."
Judges 14:1 [KJV]

As soon as Samson joined himself with Delilah his purpose in life was diverted. He was born and set apart for God, to bring about the deliverance of Israel from the hand of the

Philistines, but Samson decided to go "down" to Timnath were he saw a young Philistine lady. He did not even pray nor seek the face of God to help him. Besides, he was told by his parents not to marry any woman of the enemy tribe. "Isn't there in Israel or among your brethren a woman for you to marry? but he insisted that it must be a woman from Timnath. An Igbo proverb says *"Any grasshopper that is killed by an enemy which makes noise while approaching is at its own risk of deafness."*

CHAPTER 6

Overcoming Disappointment

When we are disappointed in relationships we should not keep blaming anybody in regret and frustration. No, we should sit down and ask ourselves some question. Was it the will of God? Was that God's promise for my life? We should know that God's gift makes rich and adds no sorrow. Therefore, any gift which comes from God will not bring sorrow. I mean it will cause no heart break or frustration.

"And we know that to them that love God all things work together for good, 'even' to them that are called according to 'his' purpose." Rom 8:28 [ASV]

At times God Himself allows some things to happen in order for us to learn from them, so we could come back to his will. This is what many people find very difficult to understand. So they hurt, retaliate and even kill one another. Maybe you may have spent a lot of money, time and resources on someone who you believed to be the will of God for you, only to be disappointed in the end.

Yes, if you are not disappointed you will never look back or even think of the bad side of the relationship or the type of choice you made. The scripture says, ***"All things work together for good to them which love God."*** Disappointment may be the best way to call you back so you can really know God's will for you. One thing is important here! God has a plan and purpose for us on this planet earth and so is working to see that we achieve it.

He wouldn't allow our future to be messed up not to talk of His plan for our life. God knows who can go with us, so we can succeed in our mission. *"Those who are the called according to his purpose"* ***"All things"***

These include everything irrespective of how it happens; its purpose is to bring us to that end which is God's plan for our life. It's for those who are the called according to his purpose. God's interest is on those who are

on His purpose list, and you are! That is the reason He will not allow you to continue a relationship that will not end well.

"In whom also we have been chosen to an inheritance,

***being predestinated according to the purpose of Him who
works all things according to the counsel of His own will,
for us to be to the praise of His glory, who previously had
trusted in Christ" Eph. 1:11-12 [MKJV]***

Remember if you fall out of the purpose of God, you fall out of destiny. Every man has a destiny, so is every woman. ***"One could go a thousand mile while two can go beyond that."*** That is the reason why we need spouses who could go with us in this marriage journey. Because two cannot walk together when there is no agreement.

Imagine a case where you are going with a wrong person on a mission, where you are expected to help each other and because both of you have a different understanding and interest about the mission, you both will find it difficult to work together in order to and interests. At times people over look these problems even when they know that they are not working together. They tend to ignore it because of self-gain and at the end they end up having a broken home. What we call ***"LOVE"*** can be a blindfold. So when you fall into it, please try to define it before it leads to blindness.

***"For I will restore health to you and I will
heal your wounds, says the Lord, because they***

*have called you an outcast, saying this is
Zion, no one seeks her"
Jeremiah 30:17[KJV]*

The usual response when a situation such as a divorce or the termination of a relationship occurs in one's life is to feel disappointed, discouraged and pained, and there's nothing wrong with that immediate emotional response. Pain is an emotion intended by God to show us that we need to start praising and thanking him so that our confidence and faith will rise up within us. The truth is, when one experiences rejection and pain in this life sometimes the memories and scars can be deep, but we will enter into strength through pain.

For our wounds to be healed and for us to receive restoration, we have to first commit our pain and anguish to the Lord. He desires to heal us of our pain. Unfortunately, most people who feel disappointed and discouraged do not turn to God. Instead they stop trusting God and start blaming Him, or they turn away from God and to other people. Hear this; the high point of a Christian's maturity is his ability to identify God's goodness out of a difficult Situation.

We have to trust God to show us how to be healed of the pain we have felt as a result of our disappointment by committing our entire situation and all our pains to Him through prayer, and then allow Him to heal us in the way that only He can.

He desires to heal us from past hurts caused by rejection; He wants us to know that He will never reject us because of our weaknesses. God is the force that can bring all the pieces in our life together.

Sometimes God allows us to go through some disappointments in order to move us from where we are to where He wants us to be. Sometimes He has to step in to rearrange our plans to prevent us from self-destruction. Remember the popular saying: ***"Every disappointment is a blessing!"*** As children of God, disappointments that we face can only be a blessing because we know that His thoughts about us are not of evil, but of peace and of joy to give us a hope and a future. (Jeremiah. 29:11)

Many a time what we think is good for us is not part of God's plan and purpose for our lives, so when relationships don't work out, rather than despair, we should trust God and praise Him because He alone knows the end from the beginning. This is why we must not leave God out of our future plans; there is no point in making plans as though

God does not exist, because the earth is the Lord's and the future lies in His hand. **Ps. 24:1-2.** Personal pain makes us vulnerable. In some cases women throw themselves into the hands of men, often times, married men, in a bid to either get at their estranged spouse, or in order to feel loved again.

The truth is, these men are opportunists who recognize the fact that the woman is at her lowest ebb, and they are out to take advantage of her vulnerability. Of all the men on earth no one can speak to our spirit or heal our wounds, just the way Jesus can. It is only

His tender love for us that can keep our mind from breaking under the pain of a disappointment; no one can comfort us or hold us like He can. One of the major lies of the Satan is that God cannot be trusted, never lose sight of the reality that the Satan is a liar. Always remember we are worthy of God's forgiveness, we deserve God's love, we have a bright future, we will fulfill God's destiny for our life, but we have to learn to believe and to trust God. Do not let the pain of the past paralyze your ability to pursue your dreams. The disappointment that you just suffered, may have run you right off the tracks in life, but faith that climbs mountains will come when you believe that God's power and your desire to get there can get you moving again.

When you hook to God's power, you will have the power to overcome the mountains of fear, loneliness, depression, rejection and loss. **John H. Vincent says,** *"Reach up as far as you can and God will reach down all the way."*

DISAPOINTMENT CAPSULES

[A] You have to allow yourself time to heal; when the hurts are deep, the healing takes time. Cry if you have to and when you want to. You will find out that you will feel better when you release pain through tears. Tears will soften your heart, wash your eyes and clear your vision, though God is not moved by your tears! Be careful in whose arms/shoulders you cry on. Crying on the shoulders of a married man would only end you in trouble and more emotional confusion and you certainly don't need that!

The fact that you have been disappointed for which ever reason does not give you the right to break or interfere with another woman's marriage, it is a sin. Don't be afraid when it comes to moral convictions, knowing what you believe and sticking by it is a sign of strength not weakness.

[B] Make the necessary changes in your life that would aid your healing process, knowing that the decisions you take will either have a positive or negative influence on the rest of your life. People decide to change when the pain of the situation is almost equal to the fear of the change. Someone once summed up: ***"put the past in the past and learn to live in the present, rehearsing yesterday's mistakes will not make living in today any easier."***

[C] Develop a plan to get through each day without spending time worrying about yesterday. You cannot change yesterday but you can plan tomorrow today. You can take up a sport, a hobby; engage in exercise, swimming, visit to the gym, reading books. You can even take a holiday break. Try to rediscover yourself, do the things that make you happy. Learn to love and admire yourself first if you have to love again.

Learn to enjoy your own company, do everything positively to regain your self-confidence, but do not look for love and acceptance and comfort in wrong places, you will only come to regret it later in life because you will be operating outside the will of God. If you intend to stay single, let it be for the right reasons. Don't do it because you once had a bad relationship or marriage and your feelings have been hurt or because you are mad at somebody.

A problem shared is a problem half solved. Learn to talk over issues with friends or family. Real friends don't bail out on you when you are faced with one of lives most difficult struggles and real friends don't judge you by your past failures. Try not to live in isolation. If you find it difficult to pray on your own, you can invite a friend to pray with you, or better still join a prayer group so that you can be lifted up in prayer constantly; there is power in agreement prayer.

You can also seek counseling at your local church or call the writer of this book. *[See the phone number at the back of the book.]* Again, you need to change your mindset from thinking negatively to positively. Confess regularly: I will be happy again, I will be fine, I am not a failure, I will experience the joy of marriage, and I will laugh again etc.

My prayer for you today is that, the Lord will give you ***"beauty for ashes, the oil of joy for mourning, the garment of praise for the spirit of heaviness."*** *[Isaiah 61:3].*
I pray that affliction will not arise in your life the second time AMEN. It's, knowing God that gives us the grace to endure pains and withstand rejection. So get to know Him, worship Him, love Him, and thank Him for your healing and your future.

However if you do not know Him yet, you need to surrender your life to Him today, so that Jesus the "healer" would heal you of all your pains and you can look forward to a bright future in Him. I encourage you to say this prayer.

Lord Jesus, I am a sinner. Please come into my life and forgive me all my sins. I believe you died for my sins and rose from the dead. Now fill me with your holy spirit and guide me from this day forward in Jesus Name. Thank you for saving and healing my wounds.

LOVE

Be careful when a man/woman tells you that ***"without you he will not marry another person in this world" or "if you did not marry him that he will die."*** Just tell the person NO and mean it. Believe me, you will find out that the same person would still fall in love to someone else and would not even die as he has said, because he/she loves his/her life more than you.

Many broken homes today were built on these sweet mouth talks which never have an end, until they test the bitter side of marriage. We Christians should know that such is no longer our language because we have passed from death to life, we are now a new creature, a brand new person, and we should not use such language to deceive our partner. It is earthly and worldly.

"Among whom we also all once lived in the lust of our
flesh, doing the desires of the flesh and of the mind, and
were by nature children of wrath, even as the rest:-- but
God, being rich in mercy, for his great love wherewith he
loved us even when we were dead through our trespasses,

made us alive together with Christ (by grace have ye been saved)," Eph. 2:3-5. [ASV]

Be sincere, tell him/her how you feel about the relationship and do not say what you know you cannot do. ***Eph. 4:24- 25.*** As Christians we should put on the new self in our conversation that which is created in God's likeness and it shows itself in true love that is upright and holy. Again when a Christian tries to hide him or herself and refuse to allow his Christian virtues to show itself in relationship, he should know that human nature cannot be suppressed because one is strong. No, it is only the spirit of God together with our spirit mixed with the word of God, confession of our faith and our belief that can suppress self and human nature.

When we ignore these instruments we become prone to sin. Human strength cannot help out in this case, if we try it we will find ourselves swimming in sin and immorality.

***"But fornication and all uncleanness or covetousness let
it not be once named among you, as becometh saints;
neither filthiness nor foolish talking, nor jesting, which
are not convenient, but rather giving of thanks. For this***

ye know that no whore monger nor unclean person, nor
covetous man who is an idolater hath any inheritance in
the kingdom of Christ and of God. Let no man deceive
you with vain words. For because of these things cometh
the wrath of God upon the children of disobedience, be
not ye therefore partaker with them". Eph. 5:3-7
[KJV]

In King James Version it says *"As becometh Saints."* Good News version *"Since you are God's people."* NIV. *"For God's holy people."* *"Let it not be once named among you,"* WHAT? Issues of sexual immorality, indecency or greed! It is not even good that it should be named at all among you before you talk of falling into it. I ask who among you started its discussion.

Why did you Many people over look its danger and close their eye, focusing on its pleasure and they go ahead to do it again and again. "No fornicator, unclean person, nor covetous man who is an idolater has inheritance in the kingdom of God." *Eph.5:5.*

ONE ACT WITH MANY IMPLICATIONS
1. When people 'fornicate' they become **fornicators.**
2. By its practice they become **unclean.**
3. By covering it they become **covetous.**
4. By loving to do it again and again it becomes an **idol.**

What is meant as a blessing to be enjoyed now becomes a curse, thereby separating them from God's inheritance. *Eph. 5:6 "Because of these the wrath of God comes on the children of disobedience."* Let no man/woman deceive you to sleep with him/her to prove your love to them before marriage. Listen, it is not even a criterion to prove a man's potency or a woman ability to conceive and bear children.

"Whose end is destruction, whose god is their belly,
and whose glory is in their shame, those
Who mind earthly things." Phil 3:19
"The angel of the LORD encampeth round about
them that fear him, and delivereth them."
Psalm
34:7"[KJV]
Such are thought which comes from the pit of hell and must be rejected. *"Be not therefore partaker with them" Eph. 5:7* have to start it? The Bible

says, ***"It should not be mentioned among you that becometh saint"*** because of its contagious power, because it is not decent that it should be mentioned at such stage in your relationship. Since you are God's people there is time for everything.

We do not do things the way others do them because we are God's holy people; it stains our holiness and makes us filthy before God and thereby makes our marriage bed to be defiled. **Heb. 13:4.** It leaves us in regret and dis-satisfaction. Fornication looks ***funny*** when it is committed but its ***implication*** last longer.

Don't seal your destiny with a man/woman whose conscience has been sealed; our conscience reminds us of the mind and will of God. When a person's conscience is sealed he/she becomes alienated from God; such person cannot please God no matter how much you preach to him/her. So I plead with you who are called saints not to be partakers with them to do evil. Have nothing to do with such people. You yourself used to be in the darkness, but since you have become the Lord's people you are in the light, so we must live like people who belong to the light.

It is the light which brings a rich harvest of every kind of goodness, righteousness and truth. Try to learn what please the Lord; have nothing to do with the worthless things that people do, things which belong to the darkness, instead bring them out to the light.

GET READY NOW

"Therefore take to yourselves the whole armor of God that you may be able to withstand in the evil day, and having done all, to stand. Therefore, stand, having your loins girded about with truth, and having on the breastplate of righteousness and your feet shod with the preparation of the gospel of peace. Above all, take the shield of faith, with which you shall be able to quench all the fiery darts of the wicked. And take the helmet of salvation, and the sword of the Spirit, which is the Word of God, praying always with all prayer and supplication in the Spirit, and watching to this very thing with all perseverance and supplication for all saints." EPHESIANS 6:13-18 [KJV]

Hey, you must get ready now. How? Put on God's armour so that when the day of temptation comes you will be able to resist the enemy's attacks. Be ready so that after fighting to the end you will still hold your ground.

1. Begin to speak the truth as a belt tied round your waist!
2. Hold righteousness as a breast plate and live in it.

3. Preach the word of God as you put on your shoes to go.

4. Hold your faith always as a shield so you can put out all the burning arrows short at you by the evil one.

5. Hold on to your salvation as a helmet.

6. Hold on to the word of God as a sword which the Holy Spirit gives you.

7. All these things must be done in prayer, asking God for His help.

Make sure you do not joke with prayer; pray on every occasion as the Spirit leads. Because of all these, be alert as a good soldier of Christ who cannot surrender to situations or circumstances and don't ever give up fighting until you have obtained the prize.

CHAPTER 7

Courtship

Courtship is a time when a man and woman get to know each other; it is crucial because it may eventually lead to marriage. The qualification of any persons to be a marriage partner is determined, hence, it is a period of critical and objective check as to whether both parties are meant to be husband and wife. Because of this, when a boy and a girl come together for the purpose of friendship [courtship] they must aim at making each other very good Christians.

This is the only way they will be enabled through the power of the Holy Spirit to add God's grace to life, multiply good morals and share the gifts of talents among their colleagues to the admiration of parents/guardians and well-wishers. When a mature boy comes in contact with a girl, and discovers she is the kind of girl he would like to have for his wife and the mother of his children, as the Holy Spirit gives direction and leading, the consent of the girl having been sought and she agrees to marry, then, with the agreement of the two families, he may begin more serious courtship.

You may like to spend more time with her. Thank God, today with your phone, you can have all the contact you need, but, where there is no phone, meeting at an open place is recommended so you could discuss more personal matters. As this is going on, there must still be no mention of sexual relationship. **1 Cor. 6:18.**

A girl could have male friends, and a boy could also know several girls in a friendly way, but it must not be intimate and a secret meeting. Every boy or girl should wait on God through prayers, as regarding the issue of marriage; you should have known that no Christian will ever make such a decision without earnest prayer to God for guidance.
Parents and relatives opinions should also be respected, although it is the boy and girl themselves who must make the final decision!

Christians, as the light of the world and the salt of the earth, are people called by God with a Holy calling so as to show forth God's praises wherever they are found and in whatever they do. Since we have many things witnessing around us, we must portray good manners in matters of courtship and marriage as shining examples for the world
to emulate. Based on all these expectations of God upon us in matters of Christian courtship the following capsules should become our point to note.

COURTSHIP CAPSULES:

[A] Courtship is not a time to gratify ones lusts, but the time to get to know the other person better. It should be a soul-spirit thing not a body -sex experience.

[B] Watch the person you are dating to know who he/she really is; if he or she has a questionable character that is against your Christian faith, reject the proposal immediately. If your reputation and integrity is important to you, then know that no courtship is worth damaging it.

[C] Darkness and light have nothing in common. Don't even imagine entering into a relationship with an unsaved person. Courtship of the unsaved person should be an exceptional race, done only with a bid that God wants such a relationship to take place.

[D] Courtship with an unsaved person is dangerous; however, great care must be applied in this direction, since courting an unsaved person is not encouraged. If you must do, be sure you are fully persuaded by the Holy Spirit of God and not use "God is leading me" here as an excuse to satisfy the lust of your sinful old nature.

[E] As a matter of principle, your heart should be allowed to guide you, bearing in mind these words, *"Finally, brethren, whatsoever things are true, whatsoever things are honorable, whatsoever things are just, whatsoever things are pure, whatsoever things are lovely, whatsoever things are of good report; if there be any virtue, and if there be any praise, think on these things." Philippians 4:8 [ASV]*

If your courtship is built on these principles, then a joyous home will be the end result of the courtship.

[F] This, you must bear in mind that a marriage partner is God's responsibility, like it is popularly stated, *"not every man is husband material and not every woman is wife."* If this is the case, then we should not force things out of His hand and thereby come settling for His permissive will. When we put our trust in God He will not allow us to be put to shame. You then must be very convinced beyond any stretch of doubt that he/she is God's choice for you.
"For I know the thoughts that I think toward you, saith Jehovah, thoughts of peace, and not of evil, to give you hope in your latter end." Jer. 29: 11 [ASV]

[G] Abstain from engaging yourself in things which will arouse you sexually. Those things may look good and you feel stimulated, but the end result will be that your moral perception will become warped. It is a subtle form of brainwashing. Take, for instance, David and Bathsheba: 11 Samuel 11:12. The king was watching over Jerusalem, maybe to see if Jerusalem gates were closed or whether their enemies were advancing against them. Good intentions you may say! But what took him there was not what he saw; rather he saw a naked woman and her beauty engaged his heart. He looked further and saw her beauty, good legs, arousing nipples, and fine back.

The message which the king received led him to inquire about her. His mind became polluted with lust that he forgot what brought him out. When a man is aroused sexually, his consciousness at that moment will be put aside and his mind will engage at the issue which aroused him. So run from every appearances of evil.

[H] I advice you, never to play with sex or the things which could lead to it during courtship because the consequences are very great. You will lose respect for each other, defeat the purpose of marriage, delay the solemnization of the marriage, risk abortion etc.

The lady may lose the man; after he has slept with her. Chances are that, if she could open her legs to him before marriage, she as well could do that to others or that she may have been doing so. It is also a form of open door to demonic operations; hence it is sin against God. Be warned! ***"Marriage is honorable in all, and the bed undefiled, but fornicators and adulterers God will judge." Heb 13:4 [RSV]***

"Now Joseph was taken down to Egypt; and Potiphar the Egyptian, a captain of high position in Pharaoh's house, got him for a price from the Ishmaelites who had taken him there. And the Lord was with Joseph, and he did well; and he was living in the house of his master the Egyptian. And his master saw that the Lord was with him, making everything he did go well. And having a high opinion of Joseph as his servant, he made him the overseer of his house and gave him control over all he had.

And from the time when he made him overseer and gave him control of all his property, the blessing of the Lord was with the Egyptian, because of Joseph; the blessing of the Lord was on all he had, in the house and in the field. And he gave Joseph control of all his property, keeping no account of anything, but only the food which was put before him. Now Joseph was very beautiful in form and face.

And after a time, his master's wife, looking on Joseph with desire, said to him, Be my lover. But he would not, and said to her, You see that my master keeps no account of what I do in his house, and has put all his property in my control; So that no one has more authority in this house than I have; he has kept nothing back from me but you, because you are his wife; how then may I do this great wrong, sinning against God? And day after day she went on requesting Joseph to come to her and be her lover, but he would not give ear to her.

Now one day he went into the house to do his work; and not one of the men of the house was inside. And pulling at his coat, she said, Come to my bed; but slipping out of his coat, he went running away." Gen. 39:1-18 [TBE]

Joseph could be taken as a good example, he had Portipher's wife on a platter of gold, but he said, "How can I do this wicked act against God?" He had little chance of being caught, but he didn't compromise. His moral perspective was God-centered. How about yours and your fellow in courtship?

[I] Do not allow your dress to speak for you; good moral can still be discovered irrespective of it's location. Many girls today have turned to using code of dressing to show how good looking or smart they are. The truth is that when you dress sexily, men will sexily look out to you, but after that what next? You cannot build marriage relationship on deceit.

I have seen men who love flashy girls, and then entered into relationship on that basis, ***"when the jungle matures, we will know who has heart."*** After parties, the man and the woman are expected to prove their worth at home, but because their marriage was built on flashy things, flashy things do not last long. ***"Ye have heard that it was said, Thou shalt not commit adultery: but I say unto you, that every one that looketh on a woman to lust after her hath committed adultery with her already in his heart." Mat. 5:27-28***

"Grace is deceitful, and beauty is vain; `But' a woman that feareth Jehovah, she shall be praised." Pro 31:30 [ASV]

Not long after their marriage, the man could not hold his peace; he said the woman had other men outside their wedlock. Another man could not tolerate his wife's inability to bear him children. Both marriages crashed and both men and their wives, who were once married, today are back to singlehood. They lost the purpose of marriage; they lost time, and of course resources and are back to zero point. May that not be your portion in Jesus name? Amen.

[J] God's way to dress, always and especially during courtship is with modesty and discretion. ***"And that women may be dressed in simple clothing, with a***

quiet and serious air; not with twisted hair and gold or jewels or robes of great price; But clothed with good works, as is right for women who are living in the fear of God." **1Tim 2:9-10 [BBE]**

Don't create room to be lusted after by how you dress or act; you will end up making people commit adultery with you in their hearts which could also manifest outside, if care is not taken. After a careful research on how to chose or know who is a marriage material and I discovered that men look out for women who have good moral and women look out for faithful men. So don't act to lure him into marring you as your attitude could cause him to lose you.

"Let not then your good be evil spoken of; for the Kingdom of God is not meat and drink; but righteousness, and peace, and joy in the Holy Ghost. Let us therefore follow after the things which make for peace and things wherewith one may edify another."
Romans 14:16-17

Therefore, know this, that beauty [which is looking good] and sexiness which causes lust are not the same thing, save your sexy skills for your future partner; it is only he who deserves it.

Conclusion

To be forewarned is to be forearmed: you have the entire amour needed to succeed in relationships with you in your hand; make use of it. *"Because I called, and you refused; I stretched out my hand, and no one paid attention; but you have despised all my advice, and would have none of my warning. I also will laugh at your trouble; I will mock when your fear comes; when your fear comes as a wasting away, and your ruin comes like a tempest when trouble and pain come upon you.*

Then they shall call upon me, and I will not answer; they shall seek me early, but they shall not find me; instead they hated knowledge and did not choose the fear of Jehovah. They would have none of my counsel; they despised all my correction and they shall eat the fruit of their own way, and be filled with their own desires. For the turning away of the simple kills them, and the ease of fools destroys them. But whoever listens to me shall dwell safely, and shall be quiet from fear of evil." *Prov. 1:24-30 [MKJV]*

A lady once said. She practiced sex before marriage, so that when she is finally married she would not be a novice to things relating to sex. I ask, the first man who dis-virgins her will still see her as a novice and will mess her up without regard for her virginity; unlike her husband who will value her and respect her for keeping herself for him.

It is better both partners learn it together and grow into doing it better and better. It is deceit to think that way. If you are already in such a situation, I beg you to come out of it; it is not a logical idea. Think of Adam and Eve, Rebecca and Isaac. Your confusion could be a condition to redirect you into your future, so don't joke with it, call now for advice. This book is addressed to all singles and those aspiring to go into married life. Buy it and give one to someone you love. You may be saving a generation.

God bless you.

ALL BIBLE QUOTATIONS ARE FROM:

New International Version(NIV), New King James Version(NKJV), Bible in Basic English (BBE), Modern King James Version (MKJV), King James Version (KJV),
Young's Literal Translation (YLT), American Standard Version (ASV), Revised Standard Version (RSV),

<u>OTHER BOOKS BY THE AUTHOR</u>

TOPIC:
JESUS CAME TO SET THE CAPTIVES FREE
https://a.co/d/hOnL5M1

Michael was destined to inherit the dark mantle of his uncle Mr. Thunder, the Chief Priest, in the feared shrine of Obiah Kingdom. Michael was being groomed to serve the spirits, he was a sealed deal for them—until a fateful trip to the city changed everything.

 There, Michael encountered Jesus Christ, and his heart awakened to a new truth. But the forces of darkness refused to let him go. He was struck by spiritual arrows, wounded and confused. He found refuge with Vincent—a stranger who welcomed him and listened to his shocking revelations about the shrine's hidden secrets and the visits of the accused servants to acquire miracle powers. Michael's battle for his soul. Did he break free from the chains of ancestral bondage, or will the forces of darkness reclaim him?

Jesus Came to Set the Captives Free is a powerful testimony of spiritual warfare, redemption, and the transformative power of Jesus Christ to save the captives.

<u>Perfect for readers who love:</u>

✓Powerful testimonies of deliverance
✓Spiritual warfare and Christian fiction
✓Inspiring stories of faith and transformation.

If you believe in the power of Jesus to break chains, this book is for you! Get your copy today and witness the battle between light and darkness.

******* "POWERFUL STORY"** *"People ought to know the devil is real and will give you what you want, but this is to the expense of your soul."*

TOPIC:
THE CATCHUMEN
kdp amazon: https://a.co/d/6jCTNrU
ASIN: B0CJVQQWC1

This is a thoughtfully crafted book that serves as a comprehensive guide to the fundamental principles and teachings of Christianity, through the lens of catechism. Designed to engage both newcomers and those seeking a deeper understanding of Christian faith, it offers a clear and accessible exploration of core beliefs, doctrines, and practices.

This follow-up guide takes you on a transformative journey, breaking down complex issues into relatable, digestible segments. It delves into the significance of catechism, revealing its role as a time-honored method for imparting Christian education and nurturing spiritual growth. Whether you are a catechumen, a lifelong believer, or someone simply curious about religious doctrine, this book provides a valuable resource for deepening your understanding of faith. It is an indispensable companion for anyone on a journey to explore, question, and strengthen their spiritual beliefs through the time-tested wisdom of catechism.

TOPIC:
THE WEAPON
kdp amazon: https://a.co/d/2zktaLv
ASIN B0CCPLYVWQ

The efficacy of weapon can be seen in its ability to pull down strongholds and help in gaining a fearless stand against opposing enemies. The battle of life is not fought with bear hands, but with spiritual armour.

You cannot imagine the amazing impact prayer through God's weapons of war had against a feeble human and spiritual enemies constantly fighting us, with the intention to destroy our livelihoods. Weapons are used to increase the efficacy and efficiency of activity. Therefore, this book details ways to engage the enemies in battle; though the use of tactical prayers that guarantees victory at the end.

TOPIC:
CHOOSING THE SEX OF YOUR BABY, GOD'S METHOD
Kdp amazon: https://a.co/d/2X6AjKe

As the pursuit of parenthood evolves, so too does the profound desire to align these decisions with one's faith, how divine guidance can help in the sacred journey of bringing forth life. Choosing the Sex of Your Baby, God's Method, is a book that sets on a thoughtful exploration to finding solution. The author through his personal experience weaves in, to bring couples who are cut in this web hope. He will take you into a realm of spiritual tapestry and weaves you in seamlessly into the intricate fabrics of family planning. To proffer solution to the struggles faced by both the devout believers and those that are not, in finding God's will and intervention in regard to having a male or female child. It's a compass to navigate through the delicate matter of fertility and prayer.

NOTE:--

www.ingramcontent.com/pod-product-compliance
Lightning Source LLC
Chambersburg PA
CBHW061256140726

47998CB00006B/2234